# Eliza

## The New Orleans Years

### 1837-1862

## Dede Wilson

MAIN STREET RAG PUBLISHING COMPANY
CHARLOTTE, NORTH CAROLINA

Cover art: Dodds/Whittington family archives
Author photo by Maurice Wilson

Also by Dede Wilson

*Glass*
*Sea of Small Fears*
*One Nightstand*

Library of Congress Control Number: 2010933616

ISBN: 978-1-59948-259-0

Produced in the United States of America

Main Street Rag
PO Box 690100
Charlotte, NC 28227
www.MainStreetRag.com

# ACKNOWLEDGMENTS

Grateful acknowledgment is made to the editors of the following publications in which these poems first appeared:

*Nimrod* (finalists for the Pablo Neruda Prize): "Papa Had Pulled Us Down, Preaching Hellfire Out of the Flask of His Mind," "*Bonsoir Danse, Soleil Couche'*," "My Captain Sets Sail" "In the French Market"
*Asheville Poetry Review*: "Morning of the Duel," "Caleb"
*Independence Boulevard*: "Christmas Eve, 1861"
*Iodine*: "My Son, My Son," "My Daughter Louise," "Black"
*Kakalak*: "Lewis, Nellie, Harrison, Thomas, Louise, Maggie, Mollie, Lillie — And Now This Wind Child"
*Main Street Rag*: "Ceremony," "My Tall Clock," "Cottage"
*New Orleans Poetry Review*: "Yellow Fever, 1853" (as "Hydra")
*South Carolina Review*: "In the Slipper-Shaped Tub"
*Spinning Words into Gold* (Maureen Ryan Griffin): "Seasons When My Feet Can't Touch the Bottom"


The author also wishes to acknowledge the immensely valuable responses of those who've read these poems, and to thank Mary Langlois for her keen eye and careful vetting of the historical details in this collection.

*For Dot-t*

# CONTENTS

# FOREWORD

Eliza Moore was born in London on August 8, 1819, the same year as Queen Victoria. Her parents were Sir Michael Moore, an Anglican minister, and his wife Elizabeth. After her father's untimely death, Eliza sailed with her mother and sisters, Maria and Louise, to New Orleans.

Caleb Alexander Parker, who had journeyed south from Sterling, Massachusetts, lived in New Orleans.

As our story begins, Eliza—who has married an English sea captain— is on board a packet ship nearing the port of New Orleans. It is late summer, 1837.

# I

## 1837-1839

## Papa Had Pulled Us Down, Preaching Hellfire
## Out of The Flask of His Mind

He was the vicar, though a slurry disgrace.
He'd reel and stutter, even weep. When the deacon
tripped over him, stone-cold in the nave, we wept,
we prayed, we buried his body, engaged
passage—and sailed. I slept at sea, as sound
as Maria and little Louise. Mum
on deck, stuffing her grief with cakes and tea.
And the captain—what did he want from me?
*My red hair. My fair skin.* I was listless,
losing horizons. He held me steady,
preened and teased. Like Papa he wore mutton chops.
I wed at sea while my sisters slept, tucked in.

# New Orleans

The smells are thicker than any in England:
coffee, sausages, sugared pecans. Flesh
too ripe, too perfumed. My own captain
unwashed—and me in sun-stained threads!
On the levee, a leper is begging.
Someone flips him a picayune. Enough,
I pray, for a dip of soup. I stumble
on rocks and cobbles, pitch through the streets.
Beg for my sisters. I saw Louise, I did,
peering back at me from a carriage.
That small bleached face. I cried to her, I ran—
my captain grabbed my sleeve. The sky is ringing
with heat and mosquitoes. I'm weak-kneed, trying
to breathe. Ah! Scents of camphor and sassafras—
that sweet reek of whisky reeling from doors.
The Vieux Carré. I sway against a wall.
He leads me by the wrist to a filthy street,
through a door, down an oily hall.

## Bonsoir Danse, Soleil Couché

"Goodbye dance, the sun is asleep."
– *slaves singing as they leave Congo Square*
*on Sunday–free day–before 9 p.m. curfew*


I slip like a wild thing into the street.
The very earth pulses and thrums with the beat
of hollow-log drums, the fling of tambourines.
Slaves raising Cain. There go the ones from Tremé—
free men of colour, heading for Congo Square.
Perhaps my captain is already there,
pinching the ginger cakes—you catch what I mean.
He'll weave home. Tease me with sleeves of pralines.
But, wait, I've gone too far. Alone. And who,
who is that staring at me? I look for shade.
Those drums—my whole body humming—

# Les Huguenots, Theatre d'Orleans

My French is so ragged! Raoul, it seems,
has challenged Saint-Bris. But where is my husband?
Said he'd find me lady-fingers, but I know
he's slipped out the door. He'll sneak in that quadroon
ballroom, stare at those women and—yes! that
ceiling that writhes, they say, with erotica.
But who is this? Who is this man, so clean
and flushed, whose cuff just brushed my sleeve?
Indeed! The one who shadowed me through the streets.

# My Captain Sets Sail

I stand on the riverbank, slapping at gnats
with my glove, air so thick I barely inhale.

And there on the quay—that man. The one
who touched my sleeve. I turn to hide my cheeks.

What must he imagine? I grieve for my captain's
absence?  I'll weep when my husband returns!

# Storms, Swells

I bite off my gloves. Throw my cape
to the floor. This room is dank and stale.
The walls are watermarked. I trace the shapes.
I'll smash anything that crawls!

I fall to the bed, burrow under the bedclothes.
The linens reek of him. I throw them aside,
lurch to the rail. Allow the sea to swallow
me—swallow me—

## Paper Tied Round a Stone
## And Found on my Balcony

I dare you in daylight to greet me.
Walk on Rue Royale. Stop anywhere.
Or shop in the market beside the square.
Look at me. You need not speak.

Caleb Parker

## Fear of Falling

The bird of sleep is dipping in and out
of dream. Men bloom like roses, climb
my balcony. Flowers deepen into faces,
those who cut me open, wounds running
warm. Who touch my hair with sleeves
of wind through living trees. One touch
so warm, so new, it transcends sleep.

# In the French Market

I walk as fast as I can, threading the stalls.
Acorn squash, late potatoes weigh my basket,
anything to roast on the grate. Yams. Cushaw.

*He's here.* I finger a sprig of sassafras.
*That man called Caleb.* I am unreeling
beneath the surface, so deep I cannot breathe.

I grip my shawl. *I'll leave.* Yes. A girl glides by
with macaroons and nougat, oranges, candied
pecans. He sidles beside, drops a silver

into the *marchande's* hand, bows to me with *figues
celestes*, sweet figs from heaven. Anyone can
see. I do not turn. I stand. I eat. I feast.

# Letter He Slipped in My Basket

My Dearest Eliza,

If—when we stand close—
I feel you are drawn to me—
as I to you—You will receive
this missive—this pitiful
nib and paper—sufficing—
for all the ways
I want to touch you—You
who belong to another—
yet are mine—

You, Eliza—you
with the flaming hair—
You I will have—

> Yours,
> Caleb

## Absinthe

From my rain-splattered balcony, I watch
this man, the one called Caleb, alone
in the *café* below. He tips his chair, lifts
a pony of absinthe. I touch my lips.
He glances away, smooths his moustache.
I lace my hands in the grillwork. A laugh
in the street. Horseshoes shuffling on cobbles.

## My Captain Returns

A hiss on the twisted tongues of this city!
Yes, I was late to the river, making
my way through the streets—rain, wind, mud and puddles,
hogs on Rue Dauphine—and late to the quay,
weaving through bales and kegs, barrels of bear oil,
hogsheads of lard. And there was my captain, face
a fury. What had he heard? I—I have done
nothing. He rocked the room with my body.
Now he is off, enraged. Somewhere Caleb waits
to challenge him. Among the blood-soaked roses
in St. Anthony's Garden, trees will weep again.

# Morning of the Duel

I unlace my shift, bend to the basin, breasts
cold against the porcelain bowl. Loosening

my braids, I lift a brush to my crown, release
the musk of my hair, its flame, its weight

warming my shoulders. My hands are numb, my breath
makes ghosts in the room. Those clattering horses!

Those smelly canals! *Now they are counting,*
*stepping away before they turn....*

# The Wait

The one who lives will want me when it is done.
What if both are dead? If both survive? Who
will enter, and what should I wear for a face?
I watch a flare from the hearth cast a shrouded
shadow. From the hall, the heft of a voice.

# After

*I did not kill him*, Caleb said.
*I found him dead, his pockets peeled,*
*body spoiled like fruit on the quay.*
*I did not kill him*, Caleb said.
*It was the crew. Believe me*, he said,
one finger pressed against my lips.

# Caleb

He dresses me, buries his face in my hair.
I grab his arm, reach for my shawl, pull him out
to the courtyard. In the oil lamp's flickering rim,
I watch the green-leafed yucca rattle its swords.
Cannons are firing the curfew. I stay him
with a touch, rip a button from his waistcoat,
hold it in my mouth to still my teeth.

# II

# 1839-1856

# Late Afternoon, Day
## of the Wedding

I skid on the slick *banquette,* my slippers
ribboned and thin. In my stays I cannot bend
but see my hem wears a rim of stain. Shackled
slaves—they say from jails— dip the smelly refuse
from ditches along the street. I hold a breath
of lavender. Between my breasts, the cold
weight of his ring. January, and horsewhips
snap. High wheels scatter mud and shadow.
A cat is sharpening her claws on a strap
of our carriage. His gloved hand lifts mine.

## Ceremony

Cold brass opens the Gothic door, painted white.
Light through yellow windows stains my sleeve. No tears
will dim his eyes, though this man I take
has trimmed his sharp goatee. The reverend's face
is oily and round, his hair in threads. His voice
falls away like footsteps down a corridor,
returns with a vow, louder than before.

Dede Wilson

# This Man

stands by the bed with his brandy, staring
at me the way a sailor stares at the sea.
The linen and trousers he wore at the wedding
opened and dropped to the floor. He breaks the combs
in my hair, crushes camellias I'd pinned there.
This heart, lashed in its corset, leaps, skips.
Unraveling ribbons, parting my skirts, he
lifts my body to the top of the riser.
I fall on him, again, again. I weep.

# Cottage

He won it, he said, in a shake of the dice.
I will not dwell on that. I touch a door,
spin like a girl, touch another. Light
will dance, ceiling to latch. I'll paste the walls

with papers—India prints, English scenes. They call
this a cottage. I call it my shining house.
*Adieu* to greasy rooms, those roustabouts
laughing and shouting outside our balcony.

I'll have a clock. Design a *partèrre*. I've longed
for green. Privet. Palm. Magnolia fuscata.
A garden of mint. A trellis of jessamine.
Mind, Caleb, my fancies don't fly from your hand.

Dede Wilson

## Alone with Caleb

*One wish.*

*Snow.*
*Oh! Scones!*

*One.*

*Papa's thumb on my wrist.*

*Eliza—!*

*My sisters! Oh,*
*Caleb, my sisters!*
*And Mum!*

*No. No. Something...*
*something I can give.*

*A clock?*

# My Tall Clock

My tall clock arrives in pieces: the inlaid
case, the face, chimes loose and ringing through my rooms.
They tell me a flatboat carried time over

the river. They say a black man carried
time over the levee, into the city,
into my halls. What can I pull from time's long

chords of truth and doubt, warm moon laughing in,
cold hands pointing out. The door opens again
and again on its impeccable hinge.

Dede Wilson

## Slaves Labor for Him

The beat of the Congo thrums through the door
with Caleb, chants of the slaves who hammer
and paint and glaze. The ones he hires, he claims,
are happy under bondage, could not make it
on their own. *Caleb,* I say, *they have a trade.*
How can I convince this man of anything?
Does he know their ways? Before a slave will sleep
he places his shoes to point straight out the door.

# Training Odette

Her hair is redder than mine, but I'll not fear
a flare at my hearth. Sassy, these Irish.
She follows me into the cellar. I point out
the cornmeal, tell her how it's water-ground
to keep it sweet, indicate she's to lift it,
carry it out. Together we'll tip the sack
into a crock. Boil water, pour it in, add
a trickle of salt. More water, cold. When done,
I'll wave her toward the cellar, explain it's best
to let it lighten overnight. She can learn
to whisk the eggs, melt butter and lard, mix in
flour, sweet cream. Oil the pan. But can I teach her
to roast snipes, pick crayfish heads, stew eels, seed
pomegranates, boil calves-feet for Caleb's
jelly—and not shake her dugs at my husband!

## Breakfast

I push the cream cheese away, its crust of brown
sugar untouched, call for Odette. *Here, take it.
How can I eat? Do you see what this is!*
I press the sheets to my breast. *A letter!
My sisters found! Mum, alive. Married again,
as I am.* How can I go to her, so filled
with child? I'll write her. Tell her to come
to me, to bring my sisters. *My sisters!*

# Letter from Wisteria Plantation

Eliza, my daughter,

I'm sending this letter with my husband's cousin — to Natchez
— down the river to New Orleans — with a prayer that it may find
you.

I walked away from you. I could not live as witness and mother.
Oh — Eliza — for you to have married the sea — that man — to
have chosen a life — of bitter rewards — much as I had done — I
suffer to think of it — Your sisters wept for you — nights — that
curious stone of a moon watching — and into the afternoons
— their small bodies wet with tears —

But ours is a fortunate tale. As I walked from the quay — a
gentleman — that lovely man we saw on our ship — the one who
stared at us! — the same small boy at his side — this man nodded
to me — and hailed a carriage. "But, sir," I said — He simply
smiled — a man with a child, after all! The carriage stopped at the
gorgeous St. Charles — and this gentleman procured three rooms
— one for me — one for Maria and Louise — one for his son
— himself — That night a heavenly supper in the dining room
— and on the morrow — this man insisted I come with him — to
Mississippi — to tutor his son. What could I say? Me — as alone as
I looked.  We boarded a steamer to Natchez — his carriage waited
to take us to Jackson —

This man — Mr. John  Armistead Whitmer — told me his story.
Two years ago he had sailed to London — for pleasure — with his
wife and three children. Once there — his wife refused to return.
She had an aunt — her mother's sister — with an estate in Surrey.
The aunt begged her to stay — with her daughters — but not her
son! So Mr. Whitmer divorced his wife — with bitterness and
loss — I cannot dream what made his wife unhappy — I gather

32                                          Dede Wilson

she had moods. The boy is difficult — why not? — deserted by his mother!

So there we were — Mr. W. and myself — suffering his lost daughters — my loss of you — a sad bond — I could not claim a spark — though I sensed this gentleman had feelings for me. My dear Eliza — what woman can remain so near a man — his clean shirts and bright cheeks — and not feel a warming? We were married by an evangelical — a Baptist! Me — widow of an Anglican —

So here I am — Mrs. John Armistead Whitmer — living in the American south — on a plantation — in this stifling heat — a darkie — yes! a slave — for me alone — a tall gentle woman who brings to my bed steaming cups of darjeeling — who irons my collars — brushes my hair — and small slaves — young girls — for each of your sisters.

Ah, Eliza — how can one conceive such a system — the heart welling with fondness and fear. We coddle our house slaves — but they tell me our overseer strikes the men in the fields — they can be intractable — And this — this dark well of humanity — is my husband's wealth! It is like theatre — the masks — and I am living it — not unhappily —

So I write you — my darling Eliza — in the hope — by some odd stroke of heaven — you have been blessed — as I have — in ways I could not dream. I pray these scribbles find you — and I may see you again in this life.

Your devoted mother,
Elizabeth Moore Whitmer

Wisteria Plantation
Jackson, Miss.

## Threat of Stings

Here in my *partèrre*, Odette is serving us
glasses of *eau sucré*, the sweet liquid
drawing bees. I fear a bee at my lips, sip
carefully, balance the glass on my belly.
Mum is out of her chaise, leaping away
from the bees. Maria is spinning under
the oak. Louise, with a net, chasing moths.
We are drowning in fragrance—mock orange, tea
olive, magnolia fuscata. Mum is annoyed
with us, eager to leave. Misses her *slaves*.
Says I must visit *her*—bring the new baby.
I look at my sisters and long for my sisters.

Dede Wilson

## In the Slipper-Shaped Tub

Odette has carried pots from the fire to top
the steaming tub. She places the fragrant
baby, fisted and warm, into my arms. Ah!
but I am healed. Dark curls spin, eyes find mine.
Against my breasts, busy heels, plumping pillows!
Sliding soapsuds over his belly, around
his legs, his buttocks, I wash him with my hands.
When he smiles I kiss him, dip him, shimmer
and kiss him, lips slipping over his wet skin.

# Men in This City Do as They Please

So who is dining with him at Moreau's?
After the high note, that one dramatic
flourish, wives are hidden behind the scrim.
Center-stage the gentlemen bow to applause.
Or drunk, unruly, play the fool—cracking
nuts in the pit, spitting across the wings.

So who is dining with him at Moreau's?
Does he regale her with tales of the river,
the way those boatmen poled around eddies, slipped
through shoals. Talk of that stagecoach, the way it swayed.
Those twittering ladies, their cage of canaries.
Does he tell her he teased the canaries?

So who is dining with him? Will he take her
out to Carrollton Gardens—swept away
by the storm? Stand entangled in the limbs
of a fallen water oak? Will he urge her
onto the levee to feel the river's surge?
Hold her—I know—too close on that slope.

Dede Wilson

## Invitation to a Houseparty
## At Blue Moss Plantation, 1849

A child in my belly, a child in my arms.
The boat tips, hits the dock. I almost drop
Louise. Caleb appears, but where's Harrison—
the child you can't let go. Lewis and Nellie
bent on the rail, watching the river, the ropes.

Strong brown hands guide me down the plank. Our boat,
La Belle Creole, surrenders its load
of oysters and oranges. Here by the river,
away from the city, I breathe again.
Breezes carry the pines in hints of resin
and green, sweep coolness out of the water.
And there is Caleb, soft curls at his nape,
gentleman, husband, papa—lurching up
the bank, seasick on brandy. Alas! Alas!

An old colored man, hair like moss, stands by a tree,
scraping a gallnut. Someone with aching teeth.

I look toward the house. Long ropes of wisteria
twist around the columns, their purple globes
like girandoles, sconces of colored glass.

How strange my children seem. Lewis is quiet
and sure, so like his father—slyly gazing
at girls. And Harrison, our mischief at three,
quietly making a road of stones. *Caleb, watch...!*
But Caleb has disappeared. Nellie's inside,
dashing from room to room. What *is* going on?
Nell's my lady of eight. Louise is screaming.

Here at dinner, two colored men pull the ropes
of the punkah, shooing flies from the table.
I'm wearing my *chiné* silk from Olympé,
green to show up my hair. Still, I feel severe.
These women gay and frivolous. How hard
they strain to make out my words, my English
accent, mixed with the city's *patois*.
I stare at Caleb, filling, refilling his glass.

After dinner, the men smoke, drink, play games
of ramps. Tomorrow they'll drink, shoot pigeons, snipes.

Caleb comes late to our bed like someone drowning.
Whatever opens between us, liquor fills.

Morning. Caleb is gone. I tug the bellrope.
Coffee appears, the woman so dark her cheeks
are blue plums. A sallow girl at her skirts.

*Is this your child?*
*Yes, missa.*
*Have you others?*
*Yes, missa.*
*How many? Five?*
*Yes, missa.*
*Seven?*
*Yes, missa.*

She can't understand me! Her girl punches
the bed, moves closer, twists her hands in the quilt.

Dede Wilson

*She have four chirren and I'se de biggest*
*and I be's five yar.*

*So what is your name, Miss Biggest?*

*Mis Bigges! That my name!*

*You're quite the talker, Miss Biggest. Can you read?*

The child looks at me. I steady my cup.
Caleb would laugh. Call it a good joke.

At breakfast the men drink juleps—brandy
with sugar, sprigs of peppermint. We feast
on meats, fish, omelettes of alligator eggs.

When we board La Belle Creole, the children
bring moss, folded sleeves of mints.  They're running
about, chewing on cane. I shoo them away.

*Caleb…*

*Yes, my Eliza?*

*Never mind. Let's watch the river.*

## Yellow Fever, 1853

Along the river levees hold the water out,
but this air feeds on water. Mosses, thresholds

swell, the Good Book thickens, sticks to your hands.
Even the woodsmoke turns in the fog

to seepage so raw the ruin will not wash out
of our sleeves. And when this fever rises

like fire in the cotton bales, it cannot be stopped.
*Mon petit chouchou*, with cheeks so pulpy and lush,

I press cool fingers against your flaming face.
*Papa! Papa! Show me how to pray!*

Dede Wilson

# Who Has Need of Hell?

My lifeless child rocks at my breast. I swoon
toward a ditch, retch. Take one step, another,
into this fester of death. Black death. Black men
with black pots, black tar to smother the rot.
Whole families dead, no one surviving to care
for their bodies, to open their vaults. I pick
my way through the streets, my baby's body
wrapped in a shawl. Everywhere, bodies. Bodies
stiffening in doorways, on porches, slipping
off carts. The awful glitter of maggots. And
buzzards, buzzards pulling ropes of gore out
of a woman's bodice. There! That mulatto,
my seamstress—much too frail to be dragging
that body, that weight.  Oh! our Pastor Clapp, two,
no, *three* small coffins falling from his cart.

# Needlework

My walls are papered in mourning.
Count the repeats. Willow weeping,
Woman bending beside an urn—
Sun on her gown, rain on her cheek.
I pull my needle through the cloth:
Same woman, same willow, same loss.

# III

# 1856-1862

## Lewis, Nellie, Harrison, Thomas, Louise, Maggie, Mollie, Lillie—And Now This Wind Child

Wind is gone though floods persist.
Anything but a hurricane!
Canals are full. They will not drain.
The streets, I'm told, are slick, a risk.

It came so quick, that bruising fist.
I wept until the fierce blows waned.
Wind is gone though floods persist.
Anything but a hurricane—

In raving dark, my ninth child came,
his cries unheard as windswirls hissed.
On trees and leaves, now, simple mist,
and I am breathing his new name.
Wind is gone. These floods persist.

*Eliza*

## Lewis Stays at the Table While Caleb Regales Him With Tales of His Journey From Sterling, Massachusetts

Listen, I was young, a man, ears flaming
with whispers, rumors, a city like Paris—
a city of mystery, whiskey, women...

Lew, you'd do the same. I packed a satchel,
leapt on a stage, with three sick ladies, their cage
of canaries. One lady slumped in her seat,
her stout, defiant sister, hands tight on that cage,
breathing through her teeth. But that mother—*Mon Dieu!*
Face like a stone, eyes a trap. I locked my jaws.

Nights no better—filthy inns, filthy linens.
Paying double for greasy meals.

And rain! Drumming against the carriage, wheels
slapping the water. After rain, we'd unsnap
the flaps, breathe the leafy cleanness of trees.
Musk of the road—scum-scents of skunk and dung.

Ah, New York, elms along the avenues.
You've heard it, Lew. We boarded a steamer
to New Brunswick. Stage to Trenton. Steamboat.
Stagecoach. Through the Alleghenies—a hundred
rapturous miles of rose, rhododendron, sumac,
vine. Even the horses silkened their pace.

I have to admit, I teased the canaries,
the ladies too sick to complain.

Dede Wilson

Wheeling, at last, and we're on the Ohio.
Finally, the Mississippi. Our steamer
skirting the surge of arks, skiffs, rafts, flatboats,
barges. Sounding, shuddering, sweeping on.
I stand at the rail, study the flatboatmen,
sleeves tied over their shoulders, bulging arms
browning like pork on a spit. You can't imagine
the ease, the way they'd skip over shallows,
wrestle the eddies, slip through cypress snags
and shoals. Outwitting the river.
No face holds like a boatman's face.

One drowned. His boat, its load of tobacco,
in flames. A lone hog floats downriver. We see
his tail, his snout, his bristly back go under.
Loss throws a pall on the water—
aromas of pipesmoke and woodsmoke.

We dock in Natchez under the bluff. People
pointing over the trees—there! an air balloon!
I run down the gangway, dash up the road.
The balloon disappears. Our boat is sounding
its bell. I've seen nothing of Natchez.

Below Baton Rouge, a canyon of pines.
We feel the pull of the river. The tops
of the cottonwoods shiver with birds. A crack!
And wild pigeons scatter like ash. That night,
that night so black, lights on the steamers
throw prisms over the water. The river
a darkened ballroom, alight with chandeliers.

Next morning, in the distance, early sun
is striking the steeples. Closer we see
thickets of masts, a choke of boats. On shore,
Indians in skins, women in rouges and plumes,
paupers in ragged regalia, juggling balls.

But, son, you live here, you know the port.

What was I seeking? Land, son. This river.
This city. This risky, randy, frivolous
city that needs but your name for a lien.
That takes a man, a man like me,
from dribbles of silver to fruits of the land.

Lewis, listen. A man makes his place, but place
makes a man. What are you now—eighteen? Nineteen?
Soon, son, this place, this city, will all be yours.

Dede Wilson

# Bell's *Crevasse*, 1858

He's off again—with Maggie and Harrison—
to stare at Bell's *crevasse*. A break in the levee
with waters so swift, two grown men, horsing
around, have slipped in the rapids and drowned.
And there go my children, skipping along that
rain-slick levee, walking too close to the breach.
Look. I know. I've seen it. Last Sunday,
beside the river at Café du Monde, we watched
the water rising, spilling into Algiers.
The little ones sitting on Caleb's shoulders.
*Me! Me!* Now they're off to the Bell place,
Caleb grinning, silly with whiskey. They say
that fishermen are working the swirls, swelling
their nets. And small boats keep rowing closer
and closer. Men! Needing to risk a *crevasse*.
And what of this city? Pity this city
where whiskey moves quicker than rivers.

# The *Grigri*

Caleb insists on a picnic. We pack
our baskets, blankets, babies—head to the pines.
Lewis, close beside me, sweeping Congo grass
out of my path. Maggie stuffing her bonnet
with knots and cones. And Harrison, running
into the woods, back, yelling for Thomas,
waving something. Louise chasing behind.

Now, this. We're home and I find them—those three—
out beyond the yucca. Hear them, first. Thomas
bent over a drum, thumping it, *dum dum dum.*
Then I see fire. Fire! Sticks blazing, circled
around a figure, a sort of doll, stitched,
stuffed with moss, no face. Louise lifting
a bowl, dark liquid swirling. *Voodoo!*

I grab Harrison. Thomas hops up, out
of my reach. I snatch the doll from Louise. *Mine!*
she cries. *My grigri! I want my grigri!*
*Harrison gave it to me!* I stomp the flames,
scream for Caleb. Lewis runs from the house,
grabs Louise, pinches Thomas by the ear.
Across the lawn, Caleb stands there, laughing.

Dede Wilson

# Caleb Tries To Explain

Can't you feel how I burn? Night after night.
The bells. The flames. Look. Last evening... You
should have seen, at least a hundred men. Steams! Pumps!
Hoses! Even so, that building flared, as though
it were stoked. Again. On Tchoupitoulas.
That same night. A liquor warehouse—destroyed.
Madeira, port—such heady smoke! I'm a man,
Eliza, a man, made for chasing blazes.

# The Bed Screw

Why should I stitch that rift in his sleeve?
Simply some threads a woman has teased.

Watching the selvages fray, instead,
I loosen the ropes that bind our bed.

## Seasons When My Feet
## Can't Touch the Bottom

Though truth will briefly light upon the surface,
little I see is clear or predictable.
My eyes are level with the glare, and water
gnats annoy my brows. A stone that cannot skip,
I hover close to drowning. I am no more
than watersnake, quick eye, quick line, divining.
Colder and colder, my lonely pond, till I
am clasped in ice. I wait for the thaw, the touch,
the break of wet lilies wild for the light.

## Luminous

We have our gas chandeliers! Light so bright
the night's alive. And we so glad to see

the last of astrals, carcels, coal oil lamps. Wick
and toil. Candles flaring while we're paring pears,

climbing stairs, trying to read. Now we can thread
our needles, sew. Children's cheeks and thimbles glow.

# My Son, My Son

*—Lewis Parker, 1840-1861*

Me! Pitying the boys in Lafayette Square—
those brassy bands, that cook Edouard with spits
and hams and clanging pans—marching north to war.
While mine—my own strong son—stayed safely home.
    *Safely home!*
To pitch from a scaffold while patching a wall.

A thump, a thump at my door, a ball, I think,
so lift the latch—and there is Caleb. Folding
his body over a body. A body! He
drops the body, knocks down a chair. My
baby! My Lew! Clods of hair cover his eyes.
His nails are blue. His feet are bare.

# Black

Lillie, merely five, with black cuffs on her sleeves.
Nellie, Louise, my little Maggie dimmed
by ribbons of dun. Dresses, sashes—even
their *pantalettes* dyed black and stripped of lace.
A year and a day in this sad dress. It's more
than the spirit can bear, to wear such emptiness.

A hundred, no, a thousand vats of black
will not bring back my son. His sisters weep.
I wear his hair woven at my throat.
I search the streets for someone with his stride.

Dede Wilson

# Christmas Eve, 1861

This is a night for drowning deep in tumblers
of darkness. I turn from the strum of the star,
fill my lungs, *fill my lungs*, with myrrh, sweet hay,
with dung. Cry to the child, that blessed son, my own,
dark-birthed as a moan's descent. Long is the wall
where I'm pinned by his thumbprint, inked in night.

# Harrison Parker

My second son is now my first, and twice
this child has run away—hot for war.
Tell me what my son is searching for.
Blood and smoke? Dagger, swagger, dice?

They've dragged him back, grabbed him by the shock
of his red hair. (It mimics mine.) They've tied
his hands, hobbled his knees, fined him, tried
to whip his horse toward home. All this he mocks.

It's not to fight for slavery. Why,
we have no slaves. A maid Margritte, Odette
long gone. Here, free blacks have slaves. Yet,
he believes in this Confederacy. Will die

for rights. I toss, grieve. See his hair
draw fire, ignite. I see him ringed in flies.
Caleb shrugs as Caleb does, shuts his eyes.
Our son's fifteen! I'll tie him to the stair.

# Our Streets are Bitter with Whispers

The Federal gunboats have run by our forts.
Caleb is livid. *Rumors*, he spits. But it's true.
Stand on our balcony. See? Cotton is flaming,
sugar spilled. Men watch from the levee, fearing
ships, Admiral Farragut nearing our city.
Not on your life. *We'll burn the town!*
One good sister at a window ledge said
she'd dump her chamber on Farragut's head.

I've buried the silver, sewn gold in my waistband.
Caleb grabs a julep cup, fills it with brandy.

# My Daughter Louise

My girl is married—and gone. She's *thirteen*,
marching to war with a man, a clerk, someone
who's sat in our parlor twice, shared one meal
at our board, who won her with sentiments
penned in that album she pressed to her breast.
At her age, life is love and love is life's own
fancy. But war, his regiment passing by—
he's dashing in to say adieu. Lou crying,
begging to marry. So Harrison runs
for the chaplain. Nellie gathers roses.
Thomas an armful of orange-blossom. Caleb
sets the chairs, fetches the Bible. The chaplain
arrives, the bride appears—in *my* lawn and lace!
Before a soul has breathed or prayed or said
farewell, the two, joined, are floating off to war.

# Solace of the Savory Pot

Shrimp on ice and oysters tight in their shells.
Margritte has fled. Caleb's drinking the day.
I'll peel these shrimp, make us an *etouffé*.
A taste of this city—before the conquering bells.

# My House, My Clock,
## My Garden of Mint

The mayor's conceded the city. I have
conceded nothing. I lift the latch, step
over my threshold. Lillie sobs and drags
on my skirts. Mollie flies out in a cartwheel

of pleasure, lands in the ferns. I point at
the yucca to warn her. Easing the baby
onto the lawn, I bend to my garden
of mint, grab and tear out the runners

the way I might tear out my hair. Savor
the rip of roots. Mollie spins beside me, tugs
at the leaves. Spearmint, peppermint, wintergreen—
scents we'll wash from our hands. I twine the leaves

through her curls, lift the baby, run in the house,
trailing green. We must be a sight. Caleb
looks up, annoyed. I laugh. Tell him I'm leaving.
Yes. Taking Tom. Lillie. Mollie. The baby.

*Leaving?* he repeats, eyes steel as a musket.

My laugh goes cold. What am I dreaming?
I lift a hand to my face, breathe in the scent.

# Eyes Opening under Water

Out of the night, the deep, the dream returns
my papa to me, slighter than a breath,
greater than the gulf between us, his tears
like prisms of glass breaking into light, strange
light, amber of brandy, silver of needles,
slim needles I know I must thread for I am
naked, owning nothing, dragging my children,
each the weight of a tear, away from Caleb,
drifting, on his river of absence.

# AFTERWORD

Eliza separated from Caleb sometime in the 1870's. She moved to California with her younger daughters and son Thomas. The 1880 San Francisco census lists Eliza living with Thomas, his wife and two children. Caleb remained in New Orleans until his death in 1891. When he died at the home of his son, Col. C. Harrison Parker, his obituary included this line: "He was much respected by those who knew him for his courage, his openness of character, his attachment to his friends and his many other stirling (sic) qualities." It says he died a widower. Not true. His absent wife outlived him by eight years. Eliza died in San Francisco in 1899, at the age of 80.

This book is historical fiction. Though the story is based on the lives of Caleb and Eliza Parker and their children, and the names and dates are accurate, many of the incidents and all of the interaction between Eliza and Caleb derive from the author's imagination. Actual events and historical truths which are woven into these poems are illuminated on the following pages.

# Behind the Scenes

## I

### "Papa Had Pulled Us Down, Preaching Hellfire Out of the Flask of His Mind"

Eliza's father, Sir Michael Moore, an Anglican minister, suffered an untimely death, presumably of alcohol. His descendants still refer to him as "the tipsy Episcopalian."

After Sir Michael's death, Eliza's mother Elizabeth sailed with her daughters—Eliza, Maria and Louise—to New Orleans. At some point, either on shipboard or soon after her arrival in America, Eliza married an English sea captain by the name of Christie. This is assumed to have been circa 1837, when Eliza was 18.

### "Bonsoir Danse, Soleil Couché"

Many slaves spent Sunday within the tall iron fence of Congo Square. The site of much revelry—drums, dancing, greased poles to climb, gunny sack races, fireworks, even air balloons—Congo Square was, and is, situated off Rampart, in what is now Louis Armstrong Park. It was the only place in the antebellum south where slaves were allowed to gather and beat their drums.

### "Les Huquenots, Theatre d'Orleans"

Theatre d'Orleans, which presented operas only in French, hosted the American premiere of Giacomo Meyerbeer's Les Huguenots. The opera house was situated on Orleans between Royal and Bourbon streets.

### "My Captain Sets Sail"

The gentleman pursuing Eliza was Caleb Alexander Parker. Caleb had journeyed south from Sterling, Massachusetts, where rumors of New Orleans—said to be as wicked and free as Paris—were hot in the ears of young men.

Dede Wilson

## "My Captain Returns"

This was the day of the *duello*. In New Orleans, it was considered a graver offense to slap a man than to challenge him to a duel. In the 1830's, most duels in the city took place at City Park, under the storied Dueling Oaks. However, duels in the French Quarter were usually arranged at Place d'Armes (now called Jackson Square) and are believed to have been fought in St. Anthony's Garden, behind St. Louis Cathedral. New Orleaneans often refer to this as Père Antoine's Garden, Père Antoine being the French translation of St. Anthony. The area was named in honor of the beloved Capuchin friar, Père Antoine de Sedella, who gardened on this site.

## "After"

Most of Eliza's descendants believe Caleb killed Eliza's husband in a duel. However, some recall being told that Caleb found the captain murdered at the hands of his crew, to whom he was indebted, before the duel could take place. Eliza appears as unsure of the truth as we are.

## II

## "Late Afternoon, Day of the Wedding"

A *banquette* was a sidewalk, usually constructed of wooden planks.

## "Ceremony"

The marriage certificate uniting Mrs. Eliza Christie and Caleb Alexander Parker on January 13, 1839, at the First Congregational Church, is signed by Dr. Theodore Clapp. Dr. Clapp lived in New Orleans more than thirty years. He is well-remembered for his fiery sermons, at first extolling slavery, though by the time he united Eliza and Caleb he was condemning the system. The gentleman from the north and the lady from England chose him for their officiating minister. Dr. Clapp is best remembered for his memoir depicting the yellow fever epidemics of the 1850's, in which he himself lost three small children.

## "This Man"

"Linen" refers to Caleb's shirt. So as not to befuddle the reader, Eliza is allowed to use the word "trousers," but she would not have said this word, and never, never the word "pants." In this era, trousers were called "limb shrouders," "unspeakables," "unutterables," and, as one might read in Melville, "nether integuments." Though a front-buttoned fly had been invented not long before this, one can only speculate on the location of the bridegroom's buttons.

## "Cottage"

A *parterre* was a border around a courtyard or the edges of a lawn.

## "Slaves Labor for Him"

Caleb was called an architect; today he'd be considered a builder or contractor. In New Orleans, Caleb was involved in the construction of the Illinois Central Railroad, the St. Louis Hotel and other buildings. In this account, Eliza and Caleb remain in New Orleans, when in fact they moved to Jackson, Mississippi, sometime after their marriage, returning to New Orleans in the late 1850's. In Jackson, Caleb owned a plantation and either owned or hired slaves who worked as builders for him. He built the Mississippi State Capitol, Hinds County Court House, and other buildings.

## "Training Odette"

In this story, Caleb and Eliza, who are living within the city of New Orleans, have hired an Irish housekeeper. Many impoverished immigrants in the city served in this manner. Though some city dwellers owned one or more slaves—and often worked alongside them—less than one percent of the area's slave owners were slave magnates, those owning more than 100 slaves. At this time, New Orleans was the third largest city in the nation with a population of 102,000. Of this number, more than 10,000 were free blacks. According to the late historian John Hope Franklin, some 3000 of these free blacks owned slaves themselves.

## "Threat of Stings"

Women often drank cool glasses of *eau sucré* (sugar water).

## "Men in This City Do as They Please"

Women were expected to go to church, raise the children, and behave properly. Most men drank incessantly, bet at the racetracks, and engaged in hot politics. Some of the wealthier men had quadroon mistresses. Some of the plantation owners and their overseers bedded with slaves. Some fought duels. Men had a voice and a vote. Eliza had red hair and a spirit to match.

Barbara Smith Bodachan, a suffragette from England and friend of George Eliot, recorded in 1857 during an extended visit to New Orleans:

> "Slavery is a greater injustice, but it is allied to the injustice of women so closely that I cannot see one without thinking of the other..."

Carrollton Gardens, a resort built in 1836 as part of what was then the city of Carrollton, followed the Mississippi River right beyond New Orleans. Paths lined with "china ball" trees beckoned picnickers and strollers. A trolley line ended at the resort.

## "Invitation to a Houseparty At Blue Moss Plantation"

A *punkah* was a huge blade hung over the dining table; slaves pulled ropes to fan the blade and shoo insects from the food.

It was against the law, at the time, to teach slaves to read or write. Eliza's response to slavery was more enlightened than most of those around her. She was from England, where slavery had been abolished in 1833, the laws slowly taking effect not long before she sailed to the American south.

## "Yellow Fever"

Between May and October, 1853, some 9000 citizens of New Orleans died in one of many yellow fever epidemics. The population, which had grown to 120,000, halved, as many who survived fled the city. This was the epidemic in which Dr. Theodore Clapp lost three small children.

## III

## "Lewis, Nellie, Harrison, Thomas, Louise, Maggie, Mollie, Lillie—And Now This Wind Child"

Eliza Parker had nine children who lived beyond infancy. On August 10, 1856—when Eliza would have been 38 years and 2 days old—a hurricane tore through New Orleans, claiming 200 lives and blowing Last Island off the map.

Here Eliza is having her last child, the one whose name remains unknown, during this storm.

## "Bell's Crevasse"

At the time, a levee break was called a *crevasse*. Bell's *crevasse* was a break "several hundred feet wide" which occurred in May, 1858, along property owned by the Bell family. In "Queen of the South, The Journal of Thomas K. Wharton," Wharton describes how the *crevasse* became a popular viewing point, and writes, "...fishermen were there with their landing nets scooping up myriads of shrimps..." and tells how some had been "drawn into the furious torrent and have not been seen since."

## "The Grigri"

A *grigri* (or *grisgris*) is a voodoo talisman, usually in the shape of a doll, believed to protect the bearer.

## "The Bed Screw"

A bed screw was a wooden screw used to tighten or loosen the ropes supporting a mattress made of feathers or straw.

## "Caleb Tries to Explain"

New Orleans was continually burning. The blaze to which Caleb refers occurred on April 9, 1860. Fire wagons pulled by horses carried steam engines that pumped the water.

The city's most devastating conflagration occurred in 1788, when some 800 dwellings were consumed on Good Friday, as it was not allowed to ring church bells on a feast day. This rule was subsequently changed.

## "My Son, My Son"

It's not known exactly how Lewis Parker died, but his uncle, Caleb's brother, also named Lewis Parker, fell from a scaffold while working for Caleb. The author has borrowed his demise for the death of Caleb and Eliza's eldest son.

## "Black"

In this era, the wearing of black for mourning was strictly followed. Custom varied according to locale but generally required a timed wearing of black for widows or widowers, followed by months of sober violets and burgundies. Children wore mourning, as well, with black trim on white garments for the youngest. With the Civil War and its terrible toll, particularly in the south, the custom of strict mourning eased and became a personal choice. Black was not worn for pleasure until early in the 20th Century. Many women wore mourning jewelry—necklaces, bracelets, brooches—woven from the hair of the dearly departed.

## "Harrison Parker"

C. (for Caleb) Harrison Parker, who kept running away at an early age to join the Confederacy, and was, each time, returned, lived to become the editor of the *New Orleans Daily Picayune* (later the *Times Picayune*) from 1881 to 1888.

Like his father Caleb, Harrison Parker fought a duel, with E.A. Burke, rival editor of *The Times Democrat*. In this instance, Col. Burke was nicked in the hip, but no one was felled. Harrison also engaged in some impromptu pistol play with Dominick O'Malley, owner of the *New Orleans Item*. Both were slightly wounded.

## "My Daughter Louise"

Eliza and Caleb's daughter Louise married Walter Wingate on April 27, 1862, and left with him for the battlefield. Walter was wounded at the Battle of Vicksburg and died a few years later. The author has Louise's first wedding ring in her possession. Eventually, Louise would marry Dr. Aaron Miller Dodds, from whom the author is descended. Louise was said to have married her first husband at thirteen, but some descendants argue that she was eighteen.

## "My House, My Clock, My Garden of Mint"

On April 26, 1862, Admiral Farragut would saunter into the city and encounter little resistance. New Orleans was taken by federal forces.

## "Eyes Opening under Water"

Eliza separated from Caleb sometime after the Civil War. She moved to California with her son Thomas and the younger children. Perhaps they were among the first to travel by railway, as the Golden Spike, connecting east to west, was driven in 1869.